Grandmother Says

J. D. Whitney

ARCTOS PRESS

Grandmother Says

ISBN 0-9725384-3-7

Library of Congress Control Number: 2004117434

Library of Congress Cataloging in Publication Data
1. Poetry 2. Whitney, J. D. – Poetry 3. North American legends – Poetry
4. United States – 21st Century – Poetry

Book design and cover paintings by Jeremy Thornton

Front cover photograph: © James H. Barker 1992. A Yup'ik Eskimo dancer Magdalene Hoelscher from Hooper Bay performing at the Cama-i dance festival in Bethel, Alaska

Back cover: author's photograph © David Junion

Inside artwork: © CB Follett and Jeremy Thornton

First Edition

ARCTOS PRESS
A HO-BEAR Publication
P.O. Box 401
Sausalito, CA 94966-0401

CB Follett: Publisher

Runes@aol.com
http://members.aol.com/runes

Published and printed in the United States of America on recycled paper.

for
> her from
> whom these
> come

for
> Gary Snyder

for
> Aroniawenrate/Peter Blue Cloud
> Antler
> Joseph Bruchac
> Louise Erdrich
> gogisgi/Carroll Arnett
> Eric Paul Shaffer
> Daniel Smith
> Denise Sweet
> Dennis Trudell
> Mark Turcotte

for
> Lisa

Thanks, for helpful support, to:
> The National Endowment for the Arts;
> The University of Wisconsin Colleges;
> The University of Wisconsin Marathon County Foundation;
> The editors of *Crone's Nest; Free Verse;*
> *GRRRRR: A Collection of Poems About Bears; Mad Blood;*
> *Northeast; Runes; Sustaining the Forest, the People, & the Spirit,* and
> *The Wisconsin Academy Review.*
> The editors/publishers of the March Street Press
> (Greensboro NC) and the Parallel Press (University of Wisconsin—
> Madison—Memorial Library), both of which published some
> of these poems in book/chapbook form.

More Praise For Grandmother Says

"Enjoyed the book & that there're still people out there writing
the real things."
 – Aroniawenrate/Peter Blue Cloud, Mohawk poet,
  author of *Clans of Many Nations* and *Elderberry Flute Song*

"good humor...good work."
 – Wendell Berry, poet, essayist, novelist,
  author of *What Are People For?*

"Wonderfully playful. I particularly enjoy the imagery and
trickster lessons."
 – Kim Blaeser, Anishinaabe (Ojibwe) poet,
  author of *Trailing You* and *Absentee Indians and Other Poems*

"amazing how it works...very valuable insights into how we need
to change."
 – Dolores La Chapelle, author of *Sacred Land, Sacred Sex,
  Rapture of the Deep*

"I think this might be fun to read to my granddaughter!"
 – Ursula K. Le Guin, author of *The Earthsea Cycle*

"I hope this book finds its way into many good hands."
 – Barry Lopez, author of *Of Wolves And Men* and
  Arctic Dreams (National Book Award)

"Marvelous poems. What an ear!! – and an eye!!"
 – Ralph J. Mills, Jr., poet and critic, author of *In Wind's Edge* and
  Each Branch

"a kind of crucial little mythopoeic breakthrough."
 – Gary Snyder, author of *The Practice of the Wild* and
  Turtle Island (Pulitzer Prize for Poetry)

A Note For Grandmother Says

In short crisp lines, off-handed and under-stated, J. D. Whitney has created a small poetic masterpiece of natural self-managing wild-world insight, with its inside jokes.

Who's this "Grandmother" Whitney is channeling, anyway? Seems like the playful spirit, life, energy of the organic world itself, an embodiment of multi-formed always-changing life; that lives whatever comes, with all the hard-won lessons and teachings.

The world is watching and listening – we sort of know that. And we halfway know that we should be alert and polite. In fact, that's what our Grandmothers taught us! So this "Grandmother" must be the spirit that teaches our Grandmothers. Watcher, trickster, analyst; wild-world-housekeeper, she spends more time with all the other critters than with humans (who are ridiculous and slightly dangerous). Grandmother plays being different beings, can be invisible, likes sex, goes beyond death.

These little games are more than old, they are ancient, and echo a heritage that is world-wide and decamillenia old. It's a rare treat to have them here in these quick sharp poems, which were in their own way hard-won. Whitney, I know, has stayed with them over many years. We are lucky he did.

– Gary Snyder

Preface

Grandmother winds her way through the stories of many Native peoples here in what we call North America – as creator, bricoleur, teacher, shape-shifter, trickster. Some would call her "mythic," a problematic term insofar as it suggests to many ears the trivial, the primitive, the quaint – a clear and costly deafness to energies larger and more important than any single writer's or speaker's, energies alive in the world we are not taught to listen to.

Although Grandmother never uses the first-person pronoun, the voice in these poems is hers. Hence the title. None of the poems here retells any existing Native story; Native peoples tell their own stories. Some such stories are, though, alluded to.

During the 500+ years since first contact, Euro-Americans have insisted that Indian peoples learn from them but have been unwilling to recognize that learning can and must occur in the opposite direction as well. Those of us of non-Native backgrounds who are learning – with the help of many people/peoples – to grow beyond the limits and distortions (some willful, some ignorant) of a Eurocentric background and education discover, as we make this recognition and let it inform our lives, that our lack of "blood" and direct cultural heritage makes in us a learning disability of sorts. Yet we find that learning *is* still possible – less wholly and quickly, but possible.

And learning to listen to those voices allows us to hear others as well – voices of the land, air, waters, and all the creatures with whom we share the wonders of Creation in which human beings are welcome but not primary. Voices. Just beyond the visible surfaces of things lies the spirit world – as it is said, "as near to us as the underside of a leaf beside the trail we walk on." Voices which, despite the insistent autism of dominant culture, we can learn to hear.

Can a man not of Native heritage learn to listen and then speak? Not *for* her, nor she through him specifically, but in the telling way of goose-honk, coyote-yip, and bear-grunt – voices here in the world to be heard by all who go outside with both ears open, voices telling stories telling stories.

Can a man not of Native heritage come to understand the world in a way, which becomes his, not in the sense of ownership but in the sense of learning?

If learning is more than just so much baggage carried in the head, if learning is, in its truest sense, what *changes* us, then what apology need be made when that learning shows itself in our work and in the ways we live our lives? But learning always brings responsibility: the need to honor what's been given – by caring for it in the shaping and telling, by sharing it, by giving thanks, and by working to resist the dominant culture's assaults on Native sovereignties and this land – Grandmother's homeground.

This is my voice. What follows is hers.

– J. D. Whitney

Table of Contents

Grandmother:

Grandmother:

Grandmother Says

Grandmother

            sits
on her sitting-down
spot on the
ground
       surrounded by
trees full of
night
       full of
ghosts
sitting on branches
speaking –
before anything was –
of things not yet
so
   saying
Old Woman Who Never Dies
tell
us
   when
the story will be
told.
Says
     saying what will
happen makes it
so.
Says
Listen.
       Says
here we go.

Grandmother

         likes

to make herself a
spider
      where
people make love.
Swings down
close.
      Fun
to watch.
They stop talking!
Good songs.
People
      all
hunched together
in the middle.
Like a spider.
          But
not enough legs.
Good try!

Grandmother

knows

better than
people
        how
they'd love
dancing
            if
they could figure
what
        to dance
to.
    But
they just stand
still
        like
trees.
Tells them:
                your
first
        lesson
is your heart.
                    Then
go visit
Prairie-
        Chicken &
Grouse.
            Do it
with your ears
                    &
walk on back
hearing
            your
own feet
            beat
on Grandmother's
back
        as you
come.
            Then
call it drum.

Grandmother

always
comes
     when
people make
fire
   &
music together.
Sits
   in the
not quite dark
beyond
     edge of
firelight
near
   where
little ones dance.
It is
their
   feet
Grandmother moves.

Grandmother

goes
walking in the world
with
nothing in it
wondering
what
needs making.
Hears
talking on the ground.
Looks everywhere.
Sees
nothing but
turds
TALKING!
saying
better
make the one who
plopped us here
better
do it
better do it
better do it now.
So
she
starts with what she's
got –
shit
& advice –
and works on
up
until:
Coyote!
Tells him
well
from
now on when
they talk
they
talk to YOU.

Grandmother

loves

good

proud

summer night

Turkey Vulture

roosting

talk.

How we don't have to

chase

OUR food.

Or flap our

wings all the time

like

those

little birds.

How we

help

Grandmother keep

house.

How we're

smart enough to

stay away

from

people –

LIVE

ones.

Grandmother

                    sneaks
real quiet
          up
behind people
when
          they
squat by water
waiting
          for fish.
Pokes them
               in
the bottom with
her stick!
          Just
to see them
leap into the
water
          like
bullfrogs.
Plop!

Grandmother

        grows
huge in the
dreams
of children –
crazy
   old
whistle-mouth
Shadow Woman
dragging
    her
hungry-bag
wearing her
necklace
of tongues
    &
little fingerbones.
Makes children
tremble
    in
sleep
   their
hands curled
tight
  beneath them.
Takes
   her
bag home
empty
   ha!
tonight.

Grandmother
             teaches
birds
     NOT
to eat
sick-making
           awful-tasting
many-legged
furbaby
       rainbow
caterpillar magic.
Says
      let them be
flowers
that fly!

Grandmother

remembers
one of her husbands.
Coyote.
Never could
trust that
fucker
but
he was hung.
Took it from a
horse
he
did.
Used it with him
good
then she
yanked it
off
&
took it back
where it
belonged.
So
much for that
husband.

Grandmother

                             likes
changing
             into
Changing Woman
changing into
                       what-
ever she
             wants
SO FAST!
             until
no one can
tell
       where
she isn't.

Grandmother
takes

her place
sitting in a
row
    of
sitting-on-a-branch
cedar
       waxwings
passing an
apple
       blossom
beak to
beak
    bird
to bird until
somebody
swallows it
down
    &
gets another
trying to
keep it
moving
      keep
it fair.
      Why
there are so
many blossoms.

Grandmother

pulls herself

up onto
end
    of
shallow-water
floating-log –
many-turtle
turtle-line
moving up
        making
room.
Suns
    her
weary
mountain-back.
        Sees
Muskrat coming
        that
look on his
face &
one hand hidden.
Says
    no
no more
Muskrat tricks
        you
let that pawful of mud
just
sink back down where it
belongs.
        Says
once was
good
    & once
was enough &
you
know it.

Grandmother

doesn't like
watching people
die.
Too much
fuss.
Oh,
what a bad
surprise!
Pah!
Bears
know how to do it.
When bears have to
die
that's
what they do.
Die.

Grandmother

                    looks
everywhere
for Wolverine
                    but he's
being invisible
again.
Tells him
            you
listen up
anyway:
            if
you scare
bear away from
what she's eating
                    then
YOU eat it all or
leave it
alone
            but don't
foul it for
everyone else.
Wolverine says
                    I'll
eat what I
like
      leave
what I don't
                &
piss on it.
Ah
      But
Grandmother
finds him
                with
her many ears.
Squats
            on that smart-
talker &
pisses.

Grandmother

lies

awake.
Too much
blackbird complaining
chatter –
how
everyone thinks
they're
just
little crows
born
to meddle.
How
it isn't
fair.
So
Grandmother puts
red
on
blackbirds' wings.
Gets her
nap
while they
fly around
showing
off.

Grandmother

          folds
her blanket
many times
        thick
to sit on
       when
she feels
      like
a long
     slow
ride on a glacier –
forward &
       back
& forward &
back
     &
back.
Hugs
    her
basketful
      of
fireflies
to warm
her
bones.
     Sings
her
   birthing songs:
for sand
for gravel
for pebble
      for
lake after lake
after lake
      after
lake.

Grandmother

watches
wolves watching
people
not
too close.
Sees wolves' eyes
wondering
if
people
were a mistake.
Wondering
if people
don't
sometimes
wonder too.
Wolves
wonder
plenty.
Grandmother
wonders
some.
But
people
don't.
Oh!
So many riddles!

Grandmother

wakes to

flying-in-her-face
dirt –
       must
be Badger
         come
to badger
        saying
sorry for the
mess
     but
nobody's perfect &
why IS my
          coat so
loose &
big enough for
two of me?
Says
     well
so you can
eat
Rattlesnake
        who
can't get his
poison
in you
       since
all he gets
is a
       mouthful
of fur.
Says
     but
don't forget
to watch your
nose.
      Says
remember
nobody's perfect.

19

Grandmother
                    hears
call of
high-
water
        fast-
water drumming on
rock
call of
spring
        toad &
frog
        song
pulling her up-
stream swimming.
Settles
down
        on her
river-bottom
gravel bed
            with
Old Man
Whisker Face.
Says
        time to
leave what we
brought
together
            so
sturgeon be
sturgeon forever.

Grandmother

tries

not to giggle &
give herself away
hiding in a
caribou

now become

food

for

little bear –

paw

holding shoulder
mouth full of
chewing on a pulling on a
tendon
THUMP

of

hoof hitting
bear on the head
pull again

thump

side-to-
side-

shaking

hard-yanking
mad-

getting

bear
thump thump thump.

Grandmother

sits under
tree full of quiet
crows.
Hides
listening.
Waits
so
long her bottom gets
sore.
Shouts
&
scares them into
air
with a
CLAP!
to hear the
sound
their
hwa-hwa-hwa
wings
make.

Grandmother

has

Coyote decide
how long
                people
should live.
Longer than
bugs
        he
says
        but
shorter
than trees.

Grandmother

sees
how people
are
afraid of what
they can't
see.
So
she
tries
making
ghosts
visible
& people get
MORE
scared.
Then
she makes those
ghosts
in-
visible again.
To
people.
Dogs
can still
see them just
fine
& they
don't even bark—
unless
they see a
mean ghost
or
an ugly one
at night
in the dark.
Then
they give
one
BIG bark:
scares
people silly.

Grandmother

hears
grumpy old
Snapping Turtle
come
up from the bottom
hissing:
I
do like these
strong jaws
but
why
this
silly tongue
I
don't like
talking
even THIS
much –
just
want to
stay in my mud
alone.
Says
be that
way if you want
but
keep your mouth
wide open &
wiggle your
tongue so fish
swim close.
Then
come
tell me how you like
that tongue.
Turtle says nothing.
Turtle
says
ahhh!

Grandmother

has

hidden

spirit

dancing ground

places

where

magic must

stay

secret.

Trusts

them

to the long

lonely

muscle

of Snake.

Says

some

rattles

are for dancing

AWAY

from.

Grandmother
                     gives
in.
    Says
ok
Coyote
      each
man can have
        a
little one like
you
    but
he'll have to
carry it
      down there
dangling
     & it
won't behave any
better
     than
you
do:
    lying
down when he
wants it
up
   &
up when he wants
it down.

Grandmother

lets
some birds wear
duck suits
because
they
like to
look like
ducks
even
if they are.
Under
those
fake duck feet
hide
duckfeet.
Behind
each duck
mask
is
Duck.
Pretending.

Grandmother

         hears
Raven
     coming
croaking about
long
    hard
no-food-to-find
winter:
      I
follow wolves
         just
like you taught me but
all
   they leave
behind is their
shit
   piles &
I
  who helped make this
world
     will
not
   eat
wolf shit –
       I
have my pride.
Grandmother
       says
pick
one.

Grandmother

                    waits

until children are
sleeping
            &
people make love.
Then she makes
THUNDER!
Wakes up the kids.
Why
        there
has to be
thunder at night.
Grandmother
knows.
            So
there won't be
too many
people.

Grandmother

        hears
honeybees coming
to ask what
they should say
        when
Bear comes wanting
honey.
Tells them
      Bear
loves you for
WHAT you &
flowers make
      but
he's so
BIG he can't
help himself
      not
help himself
      can't
help making
such a mess.
      Says
tell him to take his
sweet-
      tooth & fat
paws &
go eat berries.
      No.
Better say please.
No.
He won't listen.
Says
   who knows WHAT
will work.
      Says
that
Bear.

Grandmother

lets

nothing

stay

lost

ever.

Says

life-

light leaving

people's

eyes

never

dies

but

moves

moves

shimmers in

northern

skies

dancing

in the

face

of dark.

Grandmother

                    trots
on her bony moose legs
to play
            timberwolf
puppy game of
romping
            yipping
rolling
ring around the moose.
Lets them
            learn
to draw their circle
tight &
            sends them
scooting on
home
            in a
blast of her
Moose
            fart
thunder.

Grandmother

waits

on her high pine
branch
feathers
ruffled as
cold
wind
snow
night
falls.
Hoots
with her great horned owls
taking turns
tree by tree
hooting.
Not
much else to do.
No
cottontails
tonight.
Might as well hoot.

Grandmother

has what
looks like a
mouth
  at
the back of her
neck
  down
under her hair.
    It's
her
  other vagina.
When
men
  come on
TOO
strong
   It's
the one she lets
them enjoy.
    But
when they do
THEY
  get
pregnant.
She
  calls it her
"teaching vagina."

Grandmother

                        lies
down beside
                    Old
Man
        quiet-foot
crouching-in-the-grass
Mountain
Lion.
            Tells
him about
                    those
two-legged
people.
Says
        well
leave them alone
mostly.
            Scare
them with a
night-scream
                        if
you want
                now &
then for fun.
But
        just eat
four-leggeds
mostly.

Grandmother

<pre>
                    hides
in a nipple
aches
            to be
sucked through.
Milk river
                ride
mother to
daughter
                to
daughter's daughter &
on
    &
on through
weaves
                her
long white line.
Ties
        them
all together.
tight.
</pre>

Grandmother

waits

for Polar Bear
fussing
to stop:
I
sneak up on
seals
like
creeping
snowdrift –
push
ice-chunks
in front of me –
freeze
when they
look
but they
still see my
big
black
nose
you
should've made
white
too.
Lets
bear think.
Says
now
what
color are those
paws
&
how could they hide
that nose.
Bear
says
oh –
those.

Grandmother

                    blows
falling
          pine-
cone into
notch
          of
2-trunked
oak
          tree.
Where it
roots
          grows
nursing.

Grandmother

tries
lending dogs to
people.
Hopes
they'll
learn something.
From dogs.
But
they
still don't
sniff each other's
bottoms
don't
nibble their
itches
don't
sleep
in
nose to
tail
circles
in the sun.
Tells dogs
don't
feel bad.
Try.
Stay
as
long as you can.

Grandmother

         calls
Raven
first
  to
Deer
   lying in
spring sun
dying
    her
life's
last light
     given
to Raven
in her eyes.
How
   Raven stays
raven
black.
    How
Deer learns to fly.

Grandmother

hears
arched-back
quiet-foot
ring-tail
trouble-makers
home
from their moonlit
raid
on
sleeping-people places.
All
telling at
once:
we
scratched with our
fingers &
woke them up
& they
ran out
yelling
all
naked & furless &
how can they
tell each
other apart
they
all look alike!
Laughs at her
masked
friends
says
must be why they
all
wear
clothes in the
light.

Grandmother

                wakes

in her
       hump-shouldered
smells-bad
stands-like-a-man
shaggy-foot
coat.
      Goes
chuffing through the
honeysuckle.
              Snaps
at a butterfly.
Shits.
Slaps
       dandelions.
Scratches
          her
cranky
old
ass on a tree.

Grandmother

calls
the sitting-down
council of
all
beings –
secret
(this time)
from people.
Hears all the
wondering:
why those
two-leggeds
can't
dance in the
circle
too
why
they think they're too
good to be
food
for
anyone else
but
get to eat US.
Listens.
Says
no
no volunteers.
Thinks some.
Says
now
here –
meet your new
cousins:
Mosquito
Black Fly
bloodsucker
Wood-
tick.

Grandmother

                      finds
laughing
        breathing
rising-into-winter-night
steam
      at
beaver lodge
roof vent
         hole.
Hears
        glad talk of
water
        slapper
paddle tails
          good
for wiping tracks
               &
giving rides to kits.
How
      when she made those
two-legged people
Grandmother
            must've
run out of tails
& put
        fat on their bottoms
to hide their holes
             &
wiggle when they
walk &
drive
     each
other crazy.

Grandmother

knows

no bird wants
somebody
else's
beak
bumping its
butt
so
she has
Nuthatch creep
down
treetrunks
while
Brown
Creeper creeps
up.
Keeps
everyone –
long as they
remember
who's
up & who's
down –
happy.

Grandmother

says
sometimes
nothing.
But
what
others say
she
says back to them
again
if
she likes it.
Why
Owl
hears Echo Woman's
song
more
than people do.
Why Wolf
does too.

Grandmother

knows

those

stories about

hot

hungry

women with

teeth in their

vaginas.

How

Old Man

Coyote

or

some other

big

hero-man

comes

along with his

big stick-penis

&

cleans them out.

So men won't

have

to worry

anymore.

So those

teeth

won't

ever grow

back.

Or

so the story

goes.

Grandmother

                        tells
waddling
rustle-walker
belly-dragging
Porcupine
              little
one
     who
rises in anger
no
     you
weren't made
backwards
           all
your good stuff
on the wrong
end.
     Says
somebody
bothers you
              you
show them
ALL
you've got:
            grunt
clack your teeth
stink
     then
swat with that
fancy tail.
Says
     go ask
Skunk
       to teach you:
we go where
we want.

Grandmother

knows

how crows
always liked
laughing
                at
stories about
people
            even
before there
were
        any.
So she
made some.
                Some
crows & some
people.
            Now
they know why.
Crows
do.

Grandmother

        has
birdfeet point
the way –
       3 toes
front &
1 back
     but
Roadrunner wants
2 & 2
     to
fool
    that
following
pain-in-the-ass
Coyote.
Says
    ok.
But can't
bring herself to
tell:
   how
old
Coyote
     he can
go
  both
ways at once.

Grandmother

gives
geese
      their
shape to fly in.
Shows them
          how
to take
turns
      flying
point
      to
share the work.
Geese –
      they're
still
    grateful:
why they honk.

Grandmother

                     dreams
herself
sleek-coated
             all
glistening wet
& hot
        wanting-her-
sex-to-be-licked
Otter Woman.
Says
       this
little tongue needs
a big one.
           Says
somebody
send for that
lot-of-practice
honey-
digger
        that
Old Man
         where
is he when I need him
Bear.

Grandmother

sometimes

moves in her
sleep.
      Shifts
just a little.
Like
      bears do.
Like people.
Like
mountains.

Grandmother

                     sends
springtime
bald
      eagles
back to the nest –
wind-rocking
45
    feet
up white pine.
But that nest
                  it's
FULL
        of
little black bear
                     still
sleeping off winter.
Tells
      eagles
better wait.
Tells that
bear
      you
sleep where you
want
        dream
what you like
                     but
remember
when you wake
                     what
you can't
do.

Grandmother
                         sits
trilling in the moon-
light
          plump
& damp
                gathering
toads
toads
          to
getting bellies
rubbed
               &
story-telling
eye-
talk
        plenty
said in the
sweet
              sweet-
grass
              her
toads all her lap.

Grandmother

            hears
winter trees
exploding!
Must be
        old
nibble-lip
Windigo.
Says
      come on
in
  we'll
fatten you
up
   on
roasted
children
        but
instead
pushes HIM
into her fire.
Catches
       his
slush in a bucket
to keep
        warm until
spring
     & then
dump it out-
side
   to be
puddle
       children
can play in
safe
    until
first
frost.

Grandmother

                sings

singing it

        the

same song:

high

      deep

whale song

           bird

song

      wolf song

baby girl

          playing

with her

voice

       song

water wind & tree

song

      bee song

some people

snoring

       song

spring song

        of

peeper song

singing all to-

gether

       song to

keep the song alive

song.

Grandmother

makes

one
chipmunk
&
then another
& they're
chasing
each
other around
chirping
how
there could be
more
chipmunk
chasing if
there were more
chipmunks.
Says
that's
YOUR job.
Shows
them how.
Sends
them off
chasing
& catching &
chasing
& making
wild-
flowers
wobble.

Grandmother
                              hears
that one big
ocean
            say –
back when the world
was
        all
water –
                    make
this world
BIGGER
                    I
need more room!
So
        she
made
land
            made
LESS room for
water
                broke that
too-big-for-his-own-good
ocean
                into
many smaller ones.
And
            now there are
waves –
                    all those waters
trying to
                    get back
together
                    into
one again.

Grandmother

                    sends
her
       breath
into everything.
For
       its
time.
In
    &
out &
in.
           Taking
turns.
Out
       & in
& out.
All
life
       all
death:
           Grandmother's
moving breath.

Grandmother

asks
no-neck
short-tail
underground
                Mole
for help.
            Says
swim
        with your
big front
webbed-toe
                paddle-paws
under the skin
of earth
            where
plant-feet
            stand
in the dark.
Says
        you be
the one who cares
for them –
                be
our little
Root
Doctor.
            Mole
turning
somersaults
                in her
burrow says
yes!

Grandmother

             loves

hearing
chickadees
        sing
her
name.

Grandmother

wants

huckleberries
bad
    but
watches for
piles of
        big
bear
shit.
        Hops
around one &
oops
into another.
Knows
a trap
        when she
steps
in it.
Says
        oh!
how warm &
soft
    &
sweet!
        Wants
berries but
no
    no more
husbands.

Grandmother
                          knows
why Possum has a
forked
           penis.
Possum knows too.
People
don't.

Grandmother

slow-steps

Great
Blue
  snake-neck
walking-in-the-water
looking-for-food
hungry
   Heron.
Frogs
  say
look!
   there are
BIG fish
    here.
Fish
  say
yeah
  but
frogs
  you know
taste better.
Grandmother
grabs
  a fish
SO BIG
   she
scares
herself
  &
drops it
FAST
  to find
other fish
gone
 &
frogs gone too.

Grandmother

              peeks

in

    at

curled

coyote pup

napping

        in

old

      moose

skull.

Whispers

        through

an eye

hole:

     sleep

but not too

long –

       your

uncle got

stuck

      once

& could've

taught you what he'd

learned

     if

he had.

Grandmother

dresses

up.

Puts what her

friends

left her

when they

passed on

on.

Birch

bark.

Necklace of dried

turtle hearts.

Roots.

Feathers.

Heron

foot.

Moth-

wing powder.

Milkweed

pods.

Lichens.

Pussywillow

fur.

Her

hummingbird

skins

&

veil

of webs.

Says:

there!

Grandmother

snatches

sleeping
babies
      from their
night
beds.
      Flies
off to the woods
with them.
        Sucks
all their
juices
out
    &
fills the skin-bags
with her
      hot
breath
      around
bones
      to make
doll
babies.
      Then
she takes them
back
   &
puts them
back in their
beds
    before
morning.
      What
a surprise!
      Or
maybe this
never
happens.

Grandmother

                sits
on her rock
        by
sandy creek
bank
      looking
up
    through
sun
   -lit
maple leaf
        at
dragonfly shadows
mating.

Grandmother

                leans
back in the
hot
        hot
spring.
Watching
                her
feet
float.
        So
what if it IS
just
        Old Man
Coyote
piss.
                It
feels
so
good.

Grandmother

says

yes
  Fire
was once a
person
   she knew
because she used to
be
  that person.
When she wore her
red
dress.
    But when she
took it off
after the
dance
   it
kept on dancing
without
    her
in it.
So
  she
just lets it dance
where it
    wants
on its own.
     She
misses it
some
   but
then
   she's
still there
    in it
when it dances.

Grandmother

            laughs
hearing people fret
about
Sasquatch:
        we
don't see him
walk where he
          does
among us
        leaving
big foot-
prints
      he
moans in the
night
      he
might take our
children
      & he
smells SO
BAD!
Laughs
        wondering—
he?

Grandmother

                              says
well
          we can call you
Scarab if you
like
          or
Tumblebug –
the way you
                              work
together
                    rolling those
little balls
along
          &
down your holes.
But
     there's
no shame
                    in your
good
          big
job or
name –
                    little one
who
          never goes
hungry
               for
long:
               little
Dung
Beetle.

Grandmother
                                    gives
Mockingbird
a good
talking to
                    about
too much
talking
            in
too many voices.
Says
let
        what
other birds say
just blow
                    away
once it's been
said
once.
Ah
        now
Mockingbird's got
that
        to
talk about too.

Grandmother
                          hears
death song
of shadows
lost
      in
almost-night.
Drags
          her
bonebasket
                    goes
gathering bones –
glow
      of
moose leg
turtle
          shell
skull of beaver
skull of loon.
Sings her
basketful
                    UP
into dark
dark sky.
                    Says
bones be
light
          be
bonelight
MOON.
Says
shadows
                now
find your way home.

Grandmother

yells
turn back!
to
bears
swimming in the
little lake
toward
her
smaller island.
Sits
eating berries.
Says
there
are no berries
here!
Bears
keep swimming.
Says
bears
berries are
spoiled!
Bears keep
coming.
Says
bears
go back
now
or you'll
all be turned
into rocks!
Sits back
down
to
berries.

Grandmother

               is

Moose calf
crumpling
         dragged
down by the face
by Wolf.
Is knowing
         her
throat ripped
open
       while
still
she can.
Is
   Crow
watching.
Is
   warm-belly
full-belly
bloody-muzzle
Wolf.

Grandmother

warns
the children
NOT
        to
play with their
bellybuttons.
Pick
        that
knot loose &
all the
people
        you
can be will
leak right
            out
onto the ground
scatter
        &
run away
everywhere.
Scares them good
she does.
            For
awhile.

Grandmother

has
a twin
sister.
      Lots
of them –
some
      younger
some
older.
      Some
of them are
men.
When
      they can't
remember
who's
      who &
who's
      not –
nobody
cares.
      They
sit in a
circle
      &
keep on telling
stories
none
      of them knew.
The world
      goes
on
    as long as
they
do.

Grandmother

                      quills
her way
        toward
the end of this
world –
        when
the blanket strip
                 she's
making
        for her
buffalo robe
                gets its
last quill
in place
        then
everything's done.
But her dog
          when
she can't see him
                    he
pulls quills out
               one
at a time.
She knows
         he's
not so slow
as he seems.
              He
knows she pretends
to be
        blinder
than she is.
Thousands of years.
Still
        all who live
are here
        to hear
this story.
One more time.

Grandmother

carries

the stories –
when
       they're
not being told –
huddled in her
story-bag
whispering
       softly
among themselves:
how
    they
like changing shape
to fit
mouths
    she
sends them to
ears
    she lets
hold them
how
    they'll
always fly home –
Grandmother's
promised –
shapes
       that can
change
       but
never be lost.

Grandmother

                      says
many small birds
in trees
            never
talk too much.
Says
        she is not
now
many small
birds in trees.

J. D. Whitney, who lives on the east bank of the Wisconsin River in Nokomis/Opikwuna Bioregion with his partner Lisa Seale and their dog Animosh, teaches at the University of Wisconsin Marathon County (Wausau) and, now & then, at College of the Menominee Nation (Keshena). His previous collections include *The Nabisco Warehouse, sd, Tongues, Tracks, Mother, Hello,* and *Word of Mouth.* He has received writing fellowships from the National Endowment for the Arts and the Wisconsin Arts Board. Since the mid-1960's, he's been riding British and American motorcycles.

Half of the author's net proceeds from the sale of this book will support the scholarship fund of College of the Menominee Nation.

And the author is available for poetry readings in tribal communities and at tribal colleges at no cost beyond his immediate expenses.